Contents

Good for me

Everyone needs to eat food and drink water to live, grow and be **healthy**. All the food we eat comes from animals and plants. Fruit is food from plants.

Fruit comes in all different shapes, sizes and colours, including green apples and red cherries.

Good For Me
Fruit

Sally Hewitt

WAYLAND

Notes for Teachers and Parents

Good for Me is a series of books that looks at ways of helping children to develop a positive approach to eating. You can use the books to help children make healthy choices about what they eat and drink as an important part of a healthy lifestyle.

Look for fruit when you go shopping.
- Look at the different types of fruit in your local supermarket.
- Read the ingredients on packets to see if the food contains fruit.
- Buy something new. Have fun preparing it and eating it with children.

Talk about different food groups and how we need to eat a variety of food from each group every day.
- Fruit is packed with vitamins and minerals and fibre.
- Talk about the ways vitamins, minerals and fibre help to keep us strong and healthy.

Talk about how we feel when we are healthy and the things we can do to help us to keep healthy.
- Eat food that is good for us.
- Drink plenty of water.
- Enjoy fresh air and exercise.
- Sleep well.

First published in 2007 by Wayland
Copyright © Wayland 2007

This paperback edition published in 2009 by Wayland,
an imprint of Hachette Children's Books,
338 Euston Road
London NW1 3BH
www.hachette.co.uk

Wayland Australia
Hachette Children's Books
Level 17/207 Kent Street
Sydney NSW 2000

Produced by Tall Tree Ltd
Editor: Jon Richards
Designer: Ben Ruocco
Consultant: Sally Peters

British Library Cataloguing in Publication Data
Hewitt, Sally, 1949–
    Fruit. – (Good for me!)
    1. Fruit – Juvenile literature 2. Fruit in human nutrition
    – Juvenile literature 3. Health – Juvenile literature
    I. Title
    641.3'4

ISBN-13: 9780750259835

Printed in China

Picture credits:
Cover top Alamy/Megapress, bottom Dreamstime.com/Liz van Steenburgh,
1 and 21 centre left Dreamstime.com/Glenn Walker,
4l Dreamstime.com/Steve Degehardt, 4r Dreamstime.com,
5 Dreamstime.com/Ulina Tauer, 6 Dreamstime.com/Kathleen Melis,
7 Dreamstime.com/Magdalena Kucova, 8 Dreamstime.com/Jan Matoska,
9 Dreamstime.com/Lana Langois, 10 Dreamstime.com/Antoine Beyeler,
11 Alamy/Simon Rawles, 12 Alamy/Megapress,
13 Dreamstime.com/Juan Lobo, 14 Dreamstime.com/Marek Kosmal,
15l Dreamstime.com/Marek Tihelka, 15r Dreamstime.com,
16 Dreamstime.com, 17 Dreamstime.com/Paul Morley,
18 Dreamstime.com/Leonid Nyshko, 19 Dreamstime.com/Max Blain,
20 middle Dreamstime.com/Liz van Steenburgh, bottom left
Dreamstime.com/Melissa Dockstader, bottom middle Dreamstime.com/Tyler
Olsen, bottom right Lorna Ainger, 21 top middle Dreamstime.com/Ryan
Jorgensen, upper centre Dreamstime.com/Tyler Olson, centre right
Dreamstime.com/Pamela Hodson, centre Dreamstime.com/Andrzej Tokarski,
bottom left Dreamstime.com/Olga Lyubkina, bottom middle
Dreamstime.com/Jack Schiffer, bottom right Dreamstime.com,
23 Alamy/Megapress

You can pick your own fruit, such as strawberries, at local farms.

Fruit is grown in **orchards**, on farms and in gardens. It needs rain and sunshine to grow and become **ripe**. This means that the fruit is ready to eat.

Vitamins, minerals and fibre

Fruit is full of **vitamins** and **minerals**. Every part of your body needs vitamins and minerals to be healthy and to fight **germs**.

Eating crunchy fruit helps to keep your teeth strong and healthy.

Fruit contains natural sugar that gives you **energy**. It is also full of **fibre** that helps your body to get rid of unwanted food.

Oranges contain lots of vitamin C, which can help to stop you catching colds.

Lunch box

Squeeze fresh oranges for a healthy drink at lunchtime.

Fruit from trees

Many trees produce fruit in order to protect their **seeds**, including apples, cherries and pears. We grow fruit trees in farms, called orchards.

Cherry trees grow flowers, called blossom, before they grow fruit.

Pears and apples contain seeds inside them, which are surrounded by the hard fruit.

Fruit is juicy because it stores food for a plant's seeds. When the fruit falls from a tree, the seed inside starts to grow. The fruit gives the seed the food it needs to grow.

Lunch box

Mix together some chopped apples, chopped celery, walnuts, raisins and mayonnaise to make a Waldorf salad.

All over the world

Fruit is sent all over the world inside trucks, boats and planes. These vehicles have special fridges and freezers that keep the fruit fresh. This means that you can eat fruit that has travelled thousands of kilometres.

This pink, spiky fruit is called rambutan. It comes from Thailand.

You can eat bananas that have come from Africa, pineapples from the Philippines and kiwi fruit that has come from New Zealand.

Bananas are green and unripe when they are packed and shipped. The bananas turn yellow when they are ripe.

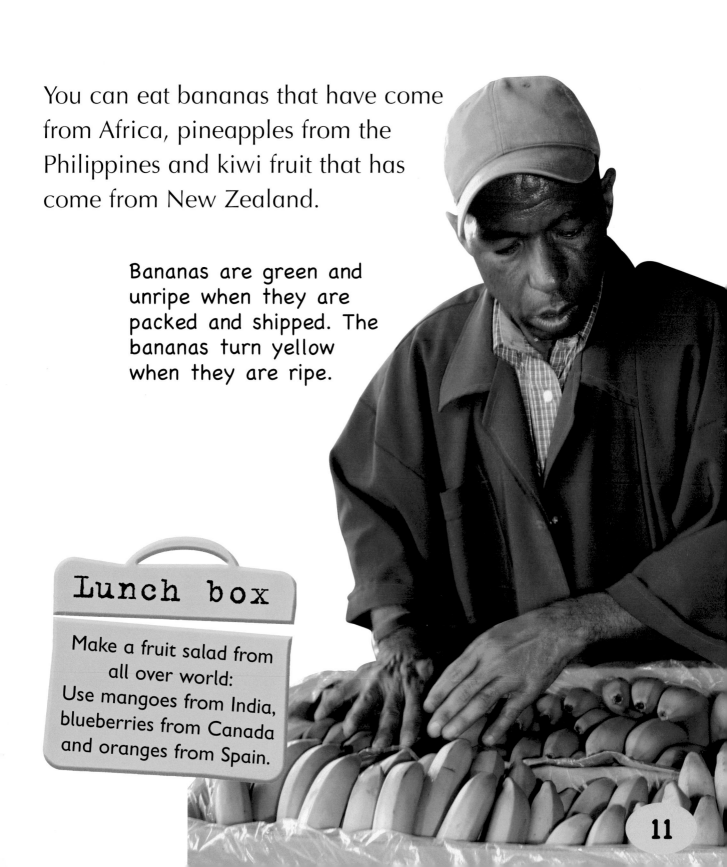

Lunch box

Make a fruit salad from all over world:
Use mangoes from India, blueberries from Canada and oranges from Spain.

Growing fruit

Fruit grows on plants of all shapes and sizes. Oranges and lemons grow on trees, while strawberries and blackberries grow on bushes.

Blackberries and blueberries grow wild in cooler countries. You can pick them off bushes, but ask an adult before you do.

Grapes grow on plants called vines. These are grown in long rows that make the grapes easy to pick.

On fruit farms, the plants are looked after as they grow. The fruit is picked by hand or by special machines.

Lunch box

Add a slice of pineapple to a cheese sandwich for your lunch box.

13

Eating fruit

Fruit has **skin** that protects it and makes it easy to carry as a snack. Some fruit has skin that is good to eat, while other fruit has skin that is too tough to chew.

Oranges are covered in a thick skin. Inside are juicy, bite-sized pieces.

Fruits of different colours contain different vitamins and minerals. Eat fruit of all colours to get as many vitamins and minerals as you can.

Lunch box

Put pieces of coloured fruit onto skewers. See how many different colours you can use.

Vitamin A for healthy skin is found in orange mangoes. A mineral called magnesium for strong bones is found in green kiwi fruit.

15

Buying and storing

We can buy fresh fruit at a greengrocer, a market or a supermarket. Fruit with tough skins, such as oranges and lemons, will keep longer than soft fruit, such as peaches or plums.

Fresh fruit is delivered to market stalls and shops every day.

Fruit can be dried in the sunshine or inside a special machine called a **dehydrator**.

Fruit can be frozen, canned or dried so that it lasts longer. Frozen fruit stored in a freezer lasts for about three months. Canned fruit will last for more than a year.

Lunch box

Add some dried fruit and slices of banana to your breakfast cereal.

Cooked fruit

Fruit needs to be cooked carefully. If fruit is cooked for too long it loses some of its goodness and will contain fewer vitamins.

Fruit can be cooked with **savoury** food. Here, chicken has been cooked with lemon.

Fruit is used to fill pies, tarts and crumbles. Fresh and dried fruit can be added to muffins and biscuits to add flavour.

Lunch box

Add apples or berries mixed with a little honey to plain yogurt for your lunch box.

Dried fruit, such as raisins and sultanas, is used to make a fruit cake.

19

Food chart

Here are some examples of food and drink that can be made using three types of fruit. Have you tried any of these?

Apple

Apple pie

Apple juice

Dried apple pieces

Orange

Orange juice

Marmalade

Orange cake

Banana

Milkshake

Banana bread

Banana split

21

A balanced diet

This chart shows you how much you can eat of each food group. The larger the area on the chart, the more of that food group you can eat. For example, you can eat a lot of fruit and vegetables, but only a little oil and sweets. Drink plenty of water every day, too.

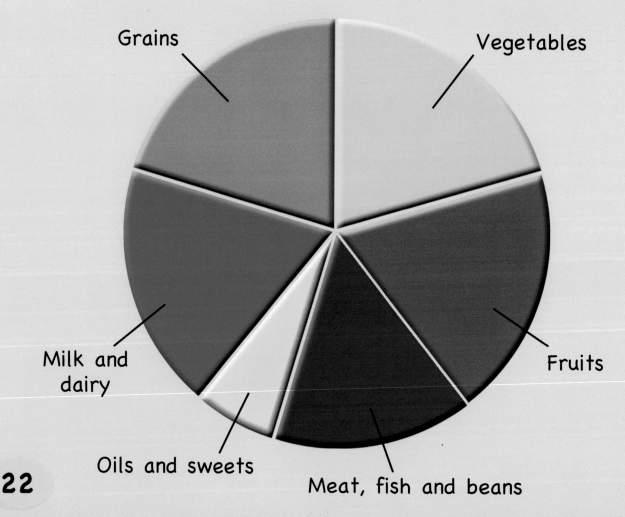

Grains

Vegetables

Milk and dairy

Fruits

Oils and sweets

Meat, fish and beans

Our bodies also need exercise to stay healthy. You should spend at least 20 minutes exercising every day so that your body stays fit and healthy.

Walking to school every day is a great way to exercise.

Glossary

Dehydrator A machine used to dry fruit.

Energy The power we need to live and grow.

Fibre The rough part of fruit. It helps your body to get rid of any unwanted food.

Germs Tiny creatures that can be harmful and can make you ill.

Healthy When you are fit and not ill.

Minerals Important substances that are found in food. Calcium is a mineral that helps to build strong bones.

Orchards Fields of fruit trees.

Ripe Something that is ready to eat.

Savoury A food that does not taste sweet.

Seeds Parts of plants that grow to form new plants.

Skin The outside layer of fruit. Oranges have a thick skin called peel. Apples have a thin skin that we can eat.

Vitamins Substances found in food that help our bodies stay healthy.

Index

Contents

KT-225-989

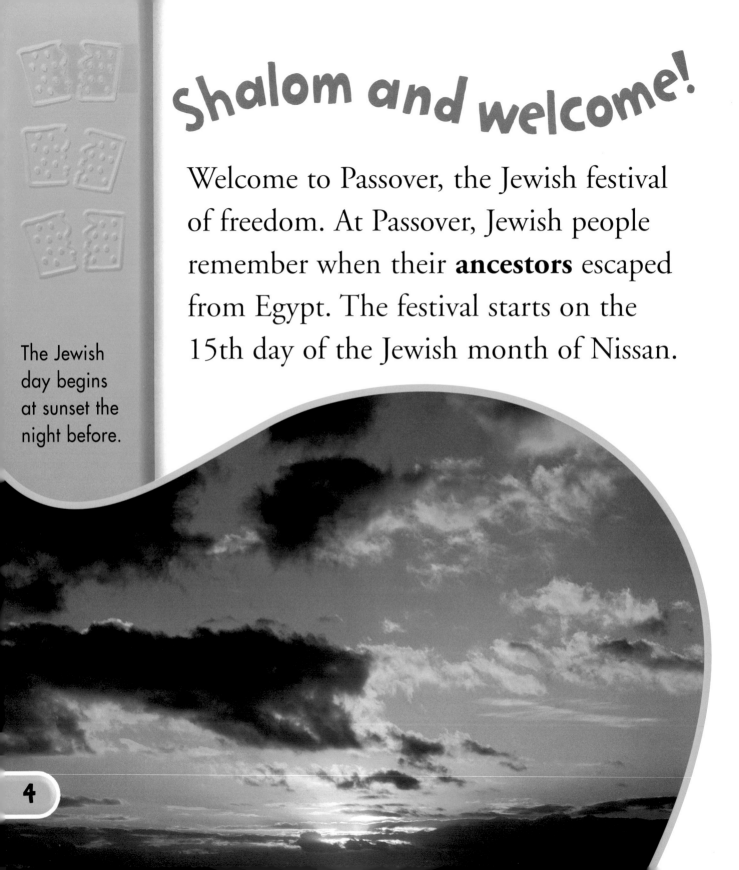

Shalom and welcome!

Welcome to Passover, the Jewish festival of freedom. At Passover, Jewish people remember when their **ancestors** escaped from Egypt. The festival starts on the 15th day of the Jewish month of Nissan.

The Jewish day begins at sunset the night before.

4

We Love PASSOVER

Saviour Pirotta

WAYLAND

Editor: Kirsty Hamilton
Senior Design Manager: Rosamund Saunders
Designer: Elaine Wilkinson

Published in Great Britain in 2006 by Wayland,
an imprint of Hachette Children's Books

Reprinted in 2007

This paperback edition published in 2009

British Library Cataloguing in Publication Data
Pirotta, Saviour
We love Passover
1.Passover - Juvenile literature
I.Title
394.2'67

ISBN: 978-0-7502-5967-5

Printed in China

Hachette Children's Books
338 Euston Road, London NW1 3BH
www.hachette.co.uk

The publishers would like to thank the following for
allowing us to reproduce their pictures in this book:

Wayland Picture Library: 6, 12, 20 / Sonia Halliday: 5, 6, 7,
11 / Corbis: title page 21, Roger Ressmeyer; 23, Philip de
Bay / Alamy: 16, Steve Allan, 10, Eitan Simanor, 22, World
Religions Photo Library; 15, Network Photographers, 18,
Photofusion Picture Library / Getty Images: 4, Baerbel
Schmidt; 17, Formula Z/S; 9, Ancient Art and Architecture /
Art Directors: 13, Juliette Soester, 14, Itzhak Genut, 19,
Helene Rogers.

DID YOU KNOW?

In Hebrew, the Jewish language, Passover is known as Pesach.

Look, the sun is setting.
A new day is beginning.
It is time
to start …

Jewish children play an important part in Passover.

5

Let my people go!

A long time ago, the Jewish people had no freedom. They were slaves in Egypt. But God wanted them to be free.

This painting shows Jewish slaves being forced to make bricks to build the **pyramids**.

A plague of locusts ate all the corn in Egypt.

He ordered a Jewish shepherd called Moses to demand their freedom but the Egyptian **Pharaoh** would not let them go. God sent ten **plagues** to punish the Egyptians.

Passed over

It took one last punishment, a tenth plague, to convince the Pharaoh to free the Jewish slaves. The eldest boy in each Egyptian house was to die.

A mysterious disease killed all the Pharaoh's farm animals.

But God told the Jewish people to mark the doors of their houses with lamb's blood. That way Death 'passed over' their houses and the Jewish children were saved.

This illustration shows a man marking his door with lamb's blood.

Freedom at last

When the Egyptians lost their eldest sons, the Pharaoh set the Jewish people free. The slaves left in such a hurry, there was no time to make bread for the journey. In the desert they baked flat loaves called **matzot**.

This baker is making dough to roll in to **matzah** for Passover.

Since then the flat loaves have become the symbol of Passover.

Matzot, like the ones these children are eating, are flat because they have no **yeast** in them.

11

cleaning out the house

No food with yeast in it is eaten during Passover. Before the festival starts, Jewish people get rid of all scraps of bread, cakes and biscuits.

Matzah and special Passover food can be found in shops before the festival.

They even clean their offices and shops. Eating only food without yeast reminds them of the Jews fleeing Egypt.

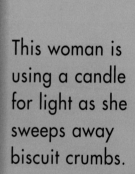

This woman is using a candle for light as she sweeps away biscuit crumbs.

13

No more yeast

The day before Passover, Jewish families do a final search in the house for food with yeast in it. If they find any, they put it in a bag and burn it.

These people are dipping their kitchen utensils in boiling water to clean them for Passover.

DID YOU KNOW?

First-born sons go without food the day before Passover, to thank God for saving the Jewish boys in Egypt.

Now the house is clean or '**kosher**'. The festival can begin.

These people have come together to burn their food with yeast in it.

15

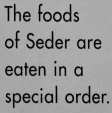

Seder food

On each of the first
two nights of Passover,
Jewish people eat a
meal called a **Seder**.

The foods
of Seder are
eaten in a
special order.

On the table is a Seder plate with different foods on it. Each item of food reminds people of something about the Jews' escape from slavery in Egypt.

Parsley dipped in salty water reminds Jewish people how much their ancestors cried.

DID YOU KNOW?

A paste of apple and walnuts is a reminder of the cement the Jewish slaves used for building.

Retelling the story

During the Seder meal, the grown-ups read out loud from the **Haggadah**, the book that tells how the Jews escaped from Egypt. The book also has songs, prayers and blessings.

These people are dipping their fingers in red wine and spilling a drop on their plates in memory of the plagues.

18

DID YOU KNOW?

The youngest child at the table asks his or her father four questions about Seder night.

This illustration is from the Haggadah. It shows the ten plagues that God sent to punish the Egyptians.

A drop of wine is spilt for each of the ten plagues. This shows how sad people are that their freedom caused the Egyptians a lot of pain and suffering.

19

Find the Matzah

During the meal, three matzot are used. A piece of the second one is hidden around the house by the parents. The child who finds it at the end of the meal gets a prize!

Children look forward to finding the hidden matzah. They share it with their family.

This family have a special silver tray on which the three matzot are placed.

21

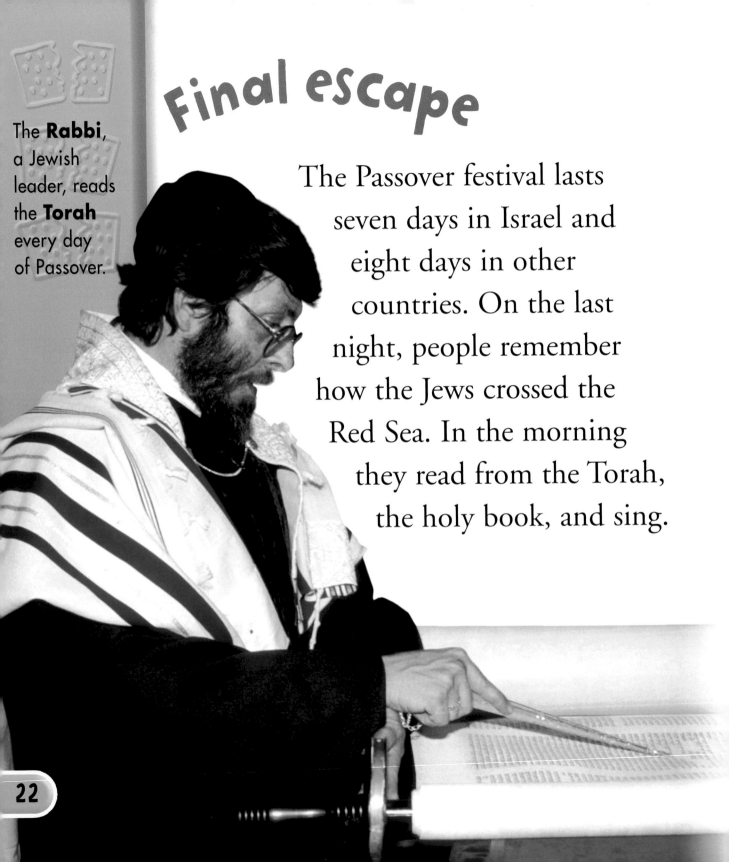

Final escape

The **Rabbi**, a Jewish leader, reads the **Torah** every day of Passover.

The Passover festival lasts seven days in Israel and eight days in other countries. On the last night, people remember how the Jews crossed the Red Sea. In the morning they read from the Torah, the holy book, and sing.

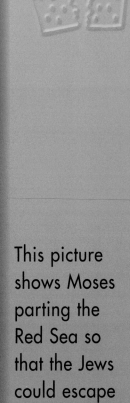

This picture shows Moses parting the Red Sea so that the Jews could escape from Egypt.

Then it's time to put away the special pots and pans. Another Passover festival is over.

23

Index and glossary

ancestors people that we are related to, from a long time ago
Haggadah the book used for telling the story of Passover
Hebrew the ancient Jewish language
kosher food that is prepared following Jewish law
matzah/matzot (plural) flat bread that is made without using yeast
Pharaoh an ancient Egyptian ruler
plague a pest or disease that spreads quickly over a wide area
pyramids ancient Egyptian tombs with sloping sides
Rabbi a Jewish leader
Seder the Jewish service and dinner at Passover
Torah the Jewish holy scrolls
yeast an ingredient used to make bread rise